HOW I BUILT A FERROCEMENT "BOULDER BUNKER"

AS SEEN ON DOOMSDAY PREPPERS

DAVID NASH

CONTENTS

PLEASE REVIEW

PREFACE

Since you are reading a book on self-reliance, I am assuming you want to know more about how to take care of yourself in disaster situations

I would like to suggest you take a moment and visit my website and YouTube channel for thousands of hours of free content related to basic preparedness concepts

Dave's Homestead Website
https://www.tngun.com

Dave's Homestead YouTube Channel
https://www.youtube.com/tngun

Shepherd Publishing
https://www.shepherdpublish.com

1

INTRODUCTION TO GEODESIC DOMES

G eodesic domes stir the imagination of people interested in self-reliance, individuals who want to built more sustainably, or just guys like me that want to DIY and don't have a lot of money.

I needed a secure storage/cabin for some land I bought to use as a "bug-out location" or, as I told my wife, a place to go camping on the weekends.

There are a lot of great reasons for building in the method I have documented.

First off, geodesic domes are amazing marvels of engineering[1], no other man-made structure covers more cubic feet for less material than a dome. They are amazingly strong, and once coated with cement, they are extremely disaster resilient.

Domes are inherently stable, and as you assemble yours, you will find that the triangles that make up the dome are under constant tension, This contributes to their strength.

This high strength and tension between the spars is important if you want to backfill over them. (However, if you want to do cover anything with tons of dirt, I would suggest you use and engineer and not plans from the internet…)

Because you don't need a lot of material to get a good amount of strength, you can build a framework out of cheap material I have had a lot of success out of using EMT conduit from the lumber store. EMT is 4-5 dollars a ten-foot stick, and the dome I built uses 35 such sticks.

Because I was building a "Bunker" for a reality show I used ferrocement, but over the years I found an even cheaper solution by the name of Latex Cement. If I had to do this again, I would replace the Ferrocement with Latex Cement, at least for the first few coats. I like ferrocement, and it is a great DIY building technique, but Latex cement is a little easier, especially for a roof.

I will go into greater detail, as well as post some pictures, however, the basics are simple:

8ft tall 16 ft diameter dome:

1. Buy 35 pieces of ¾ inch metal conduit pipe and an engineer's tape measure
2. Cut each pipe into tow pieces one 4.7 feet long the other 5.3 feet long (the engineer tape is marked in tenths of a foot instead of inches)
3. Using a hydraulic press, flatten both ends of the every pipe section. Ensure that the pipe weld is not in the center or edge of the flattened area, and that both flattened ends of each pipe are on the same plane
4. Drill a ¾ inch hole in each flattened end ½ inch from the ends
5. It is helpful to then bend the flattened ends 18 degrees out from the pipe (I just crank down on the pipe when bolting to make the ends bend where they need to go)

6. Bolt the pipes together in triangles using 2.5 inch long ¾ bolts nuts and washers (use the picture diagram in the assembly chapter to see where the long and short pipes go).
7. Cover in several layers of chicken wire
8. Mix Portland cement and sand at a 1/3 ratio of cement and sand with just enough water to get the cement to "slump"
9. Plaster over the chicken wire, either with a sprayer or using one worker inside pressing against the trowel of a worker plastering on the outside
10. Let cure over a couple days
11. Throw motlov cocktails at dome to prove it is strong…. Just kidding the producers of the reality TV show that filmed the making of this dome preferred tannerite. *Note:* due to the power of the editor, it only looks like my dad was in the "bunker" during the test phase. We don't always get along but I would never put anyone in a building and set off explosives next to it.

Dome Frequency

Domes are best described by their frequency[2]. Historically frequency is denoted by the Greek letter ν. Frequency or ν describes how many divisions are in the dome. It is easiest to think of a dome as a collection of triangles.

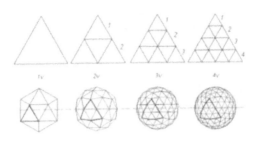

If you use a few triangles you will get something like a dome, however it will be closer to a funny looking box.

If you divide the triangle into smaller triangles and push the connections outward, you get a rounder shape. The more divisions you have the closer you get to a true dome.

If you put a dividing line in the center of the 1v triangle, it would break the 1v dome into a 2v dome.

Split it once more, you get a 3v dome.

The more you divide the stronger the dome. However, the more divisions the more complicated the math. It also means more struts of a smaller size. Basically, the more v you add, you have more strut sizes to cut.

If you stay small, a 2v dome is simple. I think it gives a good compromise of 'roundish' shape, and is still relatively simple to build. The 16 foot diameter 2v dome I describe in this book allows me to use 10 foot conduit cut into two pieces with very little waste. I needed:

- 30 4.7ft sections
- 35 5.3 ft sections

Since the EMT comes in 10 feet lengths, I only needed 35 total pieces and had 5 leftover 4.7ft pieces which I used when designing the door.

If we were building the same size dome in 3v it would need 30 2.8ft pieces, 40 40 3.28 pieces, and 50 3.30 pieces

A 6v dome needs 9 different sizes and 555 different sections. A 6v dome is much stronger, and more eye pleasing in its roundness. I wanted simple fast and cheap, so I am satisfied with my 2v dome.

Octahedron and Other Dome Types

There are different types of geodesic dome calculations, some more rounded or flatter on the base than others.

I like Octahedron domes because they are able to be perfectly split down the middle, which works good for making pavilions or starting a tunnel dome.

The icosahedron dome is based off the basic pentagon shape and is the most rounded version of the geodesic dome. Iy has a lot of smaller triangles, so it has great strength. Because of its eye pleasing roundness and high strength it is the most common version of the geodesic dome built commercially. Unfortunately, for the do-it-yourselfer, the amount of spars makes it very complicated to build.

The tetrahedron dome is least circular dome. This is because the triangles are larger and the dome is less complicated. Tt is the weakest dome shape because of this. Therefore it can support the least amount of weight. However, it is the simplest and faster to build.

You also need to understand that a dome is not exactly half a sphere (except maybe with an octahedron). Normally, they are a little more or a little less than half. This is expressed in dome calculators as being either 3/8 or 5/8 domes. In my experience, which your milage may vary, I like to build a 3/8 dome and set it on a short stem wall. A 5/8 is more than half, so it bows out toward the ground and then tightens back up at the very base. I don't like the look personally.

Calculating Dome Materials

Their are some great books on the subject of Geodesic dome math. If you are really into domes you can purchase them and learn to calculate your own sizes.

If you want to join multiple domes together to make things like tunnels you should probably learn the math.

However, there are some great calculators online that will do all the math for you. Some will even calculate things like weight of the base structure, how many square feet of covering you need, and cost.

I have a calculator link page at the end of this document that shows some of the many online calculator options and what I like about the specific sites that contain them.

Problems with Domes

I have a great out of print book called Domebook 2[3] which it, and Domebook 1, have inspired entire generations of dome builders. Lloyd Kahn[4], the author, has build a lot of domes over the years, has turned against the concepts calling them "Smart, but not Wise". He noted the following disadvantages:

- Off-the-shelf building materials (e.g., plywood, strand board) are rectangular shapes, therefore increasing waste and the cost of construction.
- Fire escapes are problematic
- Windows can cost anywhere from five to fifteen times as much as windows in conventional houses.
- Wiring costs more because of increased labor time.
- Expansion and partitioning is also difficult. It is hard to build a square wall in a round building.
- Kahn notes that domes are difficult to build with natural

materials, generally requiring plastics, etc., which are polluting and deteriorate in sunlight.

INTRODUCTION TO FERRROCEMENT

I have been interested in cheap yet effective building materials for some time. I normally focus my search on what works in developing nations, if a person with third world resources can do make something happen, then a first world inhabitant should be able to do it as well.

I stumbled upon ferrocement from researching water tanks[1]. This is a common and inexpensive method for building them. Also ferrocement has been used to build ships[2].

Basically, all ferrocement[3] is a system of mortar or cement that is applied over a thin metal mesh. Most often this mesh is several layers of chicken wire.

From wikipedia[4], I learned that it was first used in the mid 1840s in France, and it is said it is the basis for reinforced concrete.

I have been using type S mortar in my experiments, and it works well. Type S mortar has a high compressive strength and a good high-tensile bond. I like ti because it works well below grace and handles seismic and wind loads extremely well.

A good source for Ferrocement information is ferrocement.com[5], they have basic mixing proportions[6] Mixing is relatively simple as you are just making a thin shell cement covering a lot of steel. Dry measure it is 3:1 sand to cement mix.

Add water until you can draw a line in it with your finger and it the indent settles slowly. Too much water will reduce your end strength.

If you don't have access to a lot of wire mesh, or you are broke like I am when doing a lot of my experiments, you can substitute other fibers. I have had good success playing with burlap instead of chicken wire. I have also used windows screen. This is called bio-fiber, hempcrete, or burlapcrete depending on what you use.

When making my bunker, I had a lot of help from a really cool device called a Tirolessa sprayer that I got from mortarsprayer.com[7]. This site has a ton of great information as well as a blog and project advice. I could not have gotten my bunker done on time without the help of guys at this site.

What a Tirolessa is basically a steel bucket with holes at the bottom. An airline is attached to the handle and as air blows through the bottom of the bucket, it picks up the cement slurry and pushes it out of the holes. As you run out of cement, you just dip the bucket into your wheelbarrow of mix. With practice you can spray a lot of cement very quickly. The only drawback is that it takes a pretty powerful air compressor to work well.

It took us a while to find the right mix to get the results I wanted, but a mix of two parts fine sand to one part Portland cement, with enough water to give it a consistency between pea soup and oatmeal works well.

Because a mortar sprayer throws the cement out with some force, it works very well for the first layer of mix. It sticks to the frame work pretty well. After 4 or 5 thin layers the thin shell ferrocement will withstand a blow from a sledgehammer. I can stand on a roof made of this material very easily.

If you overlap your chicken wire so it makes holes about 1/4 in diameter. You can get away with 2 layers, but 4 is better. An interesting fact is that. Chicken wire and cement will expand and contract the same amount with heat and cold which allows thinner sections and less cracking over time.

There isn't a lot of hard and fast rules for ferrocement in the DIY arena. I did a lot of research to see what other people were doing and then took all the ideas and just did it. Its not really all that complicated if you are willing o do the work.

INTRODUCTION TO LATEX CEMENT

I first learned about latex roofs while researching ferrocement. While I still like ferrocement as a building material, this particular technique is a little better suited to roofs. The Dept. of Civil and Environmental Engineering, Notre Dame University[1] did an experiment on disposing of latex paint inside of cement to replace the water. This was done to find a way to use waste paint, but it had some interesting benefits.

They found the compressive strength of the cement slightly increased at relatively low latex paint rates. I am not worried about strength, I am wanting the flexibility and slight waterproofing aspects the paint brings.

What I used for Paintcrete Roofs

For my experiments I wanted cheap and easy to find. Like my ferrocement work, I used type s mortar and replaced half of the water with 100% acrylic waste paint. I started with a quart of mis-mixed paint I got on sale, but quickly ran out and had to use some leftover latex bathroom ceiling paint with an anti-mold additive.

Over time, I experimented with different paints until I found that PVA primer paint is pretty cheap and works very well in my applications. Once thing I especially like is that if you need to come back later, Old PVA based paintcrete bonds to new PVA based paintcrete. You may want to paint the old mix first with straight paint if you want a water-proof bond, but it does work.

How I Use Latex Cement

What found works the best, even if it somewhat more expensive, is to staple window screen to the frame of what I am building and then mix the cement into a high slump mix. This means it is runny. It should be able to be poured, but not soupy. Remember, the higher the liquid content is the less strong the finished product will be.

You can poured the first coat on mix on and then spread it lightly with an old broom. I find that pouring it on, lightly brushing it down and pouring new mix over covered mesh and working it down works bests. After each coat, I let it sit for several days until it feels dry. I don't let it completely cure because, for one, that would take months. Secondly, I find that it makes the layers bond better to each other.

Once I get the thickness I want, I reserve the last few layers for a very soupy mix that is mostly paint. This serves to help to coat the mortar mix already on the screen. It self levels and leaves a more waterproof coat.

In the event you want more information I have a series of videos on my site along with a PDF from the US Army Corps of Engineers of Latex Admixtures for Portland Cement[2].

If you want to go directly to the video on Youtube, here is the first three videos on my latex roof outhouse series that shows the roof, by the way, the outhouse is finished and it is quite waterproof and working well:

- https://youtu.be/nLiUigTg_nk
- https://youtu.be/oQiExZhsP4s

- https://youtu.be/dj21qJXmNGI

Additionally, I used this to make a shelter for my rabbit hutches, the more I use this technique the more I like it. Currently, I am building a bamboo based dome and plan on using this technique with burlap to build a large pavilion/outdoor kitchen dome.

PREPARING EMT CONDUIT SPARS

I have a youtube video describing the process:

- https://youtu.be/WerkFdf362A

I also have a video showing the jig and how I smashed the ends:

- https://youtu.be/RhBK4J0GgFE

Because of the math, most calculators, and the most accurate builds use tenths of an inch instead of fractions of an inch.

Being new to such a concept, it took me a while to figure out the .3 and .7 of a foot. However, I soon learned that most construction supply stores (like Lowes and Home Depot) carry a specialty engineer's tape measure. This kind of tape has the SAE measurements of ½, ¾ on one side, with the other side showing decimal feet on the other. These tapes do not cost more than traditional tape measures.

In decimal feet, instead of each foot being divided into 12 segments, a decimal foot is divided into 10 segments.

One thing to note, however you decide to measure, when you cut your struts, add whatever length your calculator gives you and add one and a half inches. This allows you to drill your holes 3/4 inch from the pipe ends and still meet your length of strut. With my dome, being the two strut lengths divided to be exactly 10 feet, I could not do this step. It still worked on a 2v dome, the finished product was just slightly smaller than the calculator length and the last few triangles were harder to connect as the entire dome had to shift to make up the difference in size.

In a dome with more frequencies, this would not work, accuracy is very important. Especially as you grow in size and frequency.

Building a Jig

To make the process easier and faster, I made a jig[1], I got the idea from desert domes, I have tried other methods, but this works the best in my opinion.

- I took an 8 foot 2×4, and marked a line down the entire length at 1/3 and 2/3 dividing it into thirds lengthways
- I set my blade at a 45 degree angle, and dropped the blade into the table saw until approximately 1/3 inch remained visible. This allowed a shallow cut.
- I set the table saw bar so that I could slice down the outer lines, and using a saw pusher for safety, I made a cuts that the farthest line on my 2x4 was at the bottom of the saw blade, and the angled cut was pointed at the center of the board.
- Next I flipped the board and ran it through again, once again ensuring the other far end of the board was at the widest part of the blade. This made a shallow 'v' shaped cut.
- Once I removed the long triangular waste piece, I cut the board at 6 foot and screwed a section of 2×4 to the end to act as a stopper.
- Lastly, I measured and marked two lines at 4.7 inches and 5.3

inches from the stopper. This allowed me to make exact marks on each pipe to ensure they were all cut the same length.

Cutting the Spars

You can use a hacksaw, but I found a LARGE pipe cutter was much easier. The larger the better, and a pipe cutter made it easy to get exacting cuts.

Once all the pipes were cut, I then took a sharpie and marked the weld lines, and a mark about an inch and a half from each end.

Once all of the pipes were cut and marked I was ready to change my jig around and get into the smashing[2] and drilling of the ends of the pipe.

Flattening the Ends of the Spars

I have read that you should not have the weld in the center or on the side of your flattened end. If you drill through the weld it can cause the end it to crack. Since I took the step of marking the weld I simply rotated it 45 degrees from the press and it ended up about 1/3 of the way on the flat end.

There are many ways you can flatten the strut ends: You can hammer them flat, use a large shop vice (reportedly this is destructive to the vice), or use a hydraulic press. I tried them all and decided to use a shop press. I saved up and bought a 12 ton press specifically to make domes. It works well, but I want to add a hydraulic jack instead of a hand pumped jack to save time when making these domes.

I used a sawhorse to set my 2×4 jig parallel to the ground when I had one end of the jug stationed under the end of the press.

I modified my jig and thinned down one end about 4.1 inches from the stop. This allowed me to place one arbor plate on the 2×4 and line up one end of the plate with the line I marked 1.5 inches from the end

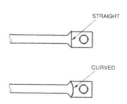

That way, each pipe was smashed the exact same amount. Using the arbor plate also allowed me to smash the end with a curve, instead of straight across. This makes each end stronger.

On the desert domes site, they smashed one end of every piece of conduit, drilled it, and then used a bolt screwed into the jig to ensure the other end got flattened on the same plane.

I tried that on the first 10, but found that it was easier and faster if I smashed one end, flipped it over, laid it in the grove, and carefully smashed the other end. I did take the time to ensure that I only smashed the second end after ensuring that everything was lined up and the flat ends were on the same plane. It was not exact, but it was MUCH easier.

Drilling Holes

Once the ends were smashed, I took down the jig, and set it on my drill press, clamped the jig down, and ensured that the hole would be drilled in the center of the flattened conduit end ¾ of an inch from the end.

I used high quality titanium drill bits. This wears out drill bits, my dome used up 2 bits to drill the 130 holes.

Bending the Struts

The triangles don't blot together flat. They bend to make a dome. Most calculators give you the correct angles to bed the ends of your spars. However, I find that in real life the accuracy of the bends is not really important, at least not as important as the length between bolt holes.

In real life, I crank down on the nuts and bolts (using washers so I don't pull through the conduit ends), and the correct angles naturally appear.

Of course, this makes the last few triangles difficult to fit together. To make that process easier, I put everything together very loose, with only a thread or two threaded into the nuts. When I tighten the nuts at the end of the construction cycle I do it in series like putting on a car tire.

However, if you want to come correct, I will add the accurate bending angles for the specific frequencies of domes.

The bending angles[3] are as follows:

- 1v dome: bend 32° on each end
- 2v dome: bend A's 18°, and B's 16° on each end
- 3v dome: bend A's 10°, B's and C's 12° on each end
- 4v dome: bend all struts 7°-9° on each end
- 5v dome: bend all struts 6°-7° on each end
- 6v dome: bend all struts 5°-6° on each end

Painting

Once all the pipes were drilled I painted the ends. I did this to prevent rust where I drilled through the zinc coating, However, the real value was identifying the different lengths of pipe during assembly.

5

ASSEMBLING THE BASIC DOME

I made a Youtube video of the Assembly that you can watch here:

- https://youtu.be/R4Vy8FiOFY8

When I made my first dome I found a great assembly diagram on Mike's Spacetime. This site no longer has the diagram, but here is a representative work.

The diagram uses Green and Black for the struts as white doesn't show up on paper, but I used white and black paint

Black designates the long studs in this 2v dome. In this case they are 5.3 feet long.

The Green lines in the diagram represent the short lengths, and they are all 4.3 feet long.

As I said in earlier sections you will need 35 black sections and 20

Green/White sections. I always print this page or draw a large version to nail somewhere near building. The production crew for my Doomsday prepper episode liked the redneckedness of a hand drawn paper nailed to a tree.

I have heard that some people start at the bottom and work up, but in my experience I find starting at the top and working down works best for me.

If you look carefully you will see that a 2v dome is 6 pentagons bolted together, its not assembled that way, but knowing that might make it easier to visualize.

Note: My dad wants me to get a contractor license and allow him to build these domes commercially. I am not interested in the exactness building for pay would require, but if I was to do this, I would build a lot of these pentagons and attach them together and use as a removable form. Similar to how monolithic domes[1] use air forms to build domes.

To start, take 5 short struts and bolt them together.

Next take 5 long struts and bolt them to the free ends of your short struts.

Keep everything loose, because as you get closer to having all the short struts bolted to the long struts the center vertices of 5 short struts will have to bow outward.

At each corner of your pentagon, lay out 2 long and one short strut. (Keep the short strut between the two longer struts.)

Now, taking each corner at a time, unbolt a corner and add the black-green-black struts, and bolt.

Don't tighten the bolts; it is much easier if you keep everything loose until ALL the struts are connected.

If you start at a corner, you will notice that the struts are in the pattern 2 black, 1 green, two black, 1 green. Continue this all the way around. Bolt the side by side black struts together. You will have 5 triangles and 5 short struts radiating out from your pentagon.

LAY OUT 10 short struts around your dome.

Bolt two to the point of each triangle you made in the last step.

Next bolt the free ends of the struts to the short struts from the last step.

As you do this the structure will start to "stand up". I found that it is easier if you have help to lift the top of the structure up, freeing me to pull the struts together.

THIS PART CAN GET a little complicated so feel free to look at the diagram as much as needed.

For the next step you will need 10 long struts and 10 short struts.

Look at the base of structure at each bolt and you will either see 3 short struts (green/white) bolted together OR 2 long struts (black) connected to 2 short (green/white) struts.

At every position with the three short struts lay down 2 more short struts.

At every position where there are 4 struts (2 long, 2 short) lay down 2 long black struts.

Bolt them together in the same way you have done in all the previous steps. Knowing that by this time the dome is wanting to stand up.

I have learned that you can do this by yourself, but extra hands makes this MUCH easier. The first time I built this type of dome, my wife and I put the frame together in about 30 minutes, and she doesn't know the difference in a wrench and a ratchet.

Lastly lay out the last 10 long struts around the base.

These 10 black struts are your base. I find it easiest to start by connecting a short and long strut from the previous step and making a triangle with one of the base struts coming off each side. I then skip the next long and short struts and repeat.

That way I can control the lifting of the dome, and I don't have to lift the entire 150 pounds of conduit pipe each time.

As you come back and connect the struts you skipped, take particular car to ensure that center of each pentagon of short struts is pushed outwards. When we did this the first time, I did not look, and some were pushed inward causing me to have to unbolt entire sections to fix it.

Once everything is assembled you can now tighten the bolts.

You will find that at each vertex (connection) the dome is incredibly strong, however, remember it is only thin walled conduit. The individual pipes are not that strong. I can easily climb the structure if I stay at the connections. I did a pull up in the center of a bar and the bar readily bent.

Remember to stake down the dome, especially if it is a temporary structure using a tarp or parachute covering. The frame is light and will easily blow away.

I did not use any foundation with my dome, which I knew was a mistake, but I was in a hurry to prepare the site for filming.

My later domes are set on some kind of foundation. I like using cinder blocks with a cap block on the bottom and top of the larger block and set over a rubble trench, this allows me to build a wooden floor with a significant gap between the ground and the bottom of the dome. If you do this and allow a small hole at the top of the dome it makes a weird cooling system, which Fuller discovered by accident and explained[2]. This concept is used in nuclear power plants cooling towers.

6

BUILDING A DOOR

V ideo explaining the door:

- https://youtu.be/rK1F4iVu87k

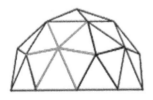

When figuring out the door I got the basic idea from my test build in my front yard, but when my Dad came to help me build the actual cement dome he brought a lifetime of construction experience that I just don't have.

We fiddled around and came up with an idea that I am very happy with but it worked. Unfortunately, due to the time constraints of the film crew we did not write down any measurements, and I could not take video of it.

It has been a main problem with domes to figure out doors. A lot of very popular wood frame construction guides for building a geodome spend a lot of time with how to cut the wooded spars and build the domes, but then totally ignore the door.

However, with the pictures I made on the computer and the experience you will have building the dome, I am sure you can figure it out.

Besides the dome itself, you will need one of the extra 4.3 foot struts, some plumber strap, some nails, and 2x6 boards for the door frame.

We will be working with one of the pentagons.

Pick one that faces the direction you want your door to face (lift the dome and rotate it if needed)

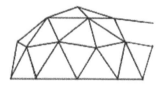

Unbolt the center bolt. Loosed, but do not remove the bolts on the other ends of the struts making the pentagon.

Next, bend the struts outward, as shown in the picture to the left.

Connect the 6 struts into 3 triangles, one at the top, and one on each side of the doorway.

If you want to measure and cut extra conduit you can connect the triangles, but we are just using this to connect to a wood door frame, and are going to wrap welded wire fence over the wood, we elected to leave the triangles "loose".

Frame in the door using traditional carpentry techniques.

We attached the door frame to the conduit pipe using galvanized pipe strapping tape.

We also did not follow this picture exactly, as we did not attach the top 2 struts to the corner, but made a triangle that stuck out about 8 inches from the center of the door frame. My goal is to use this to attach a security camera or light to this, as well as to make a small overhang to reduce rain on whoever is unlocking the door.

This picture shows the rough process, we had not leveled the frame yet, nor finished wrapping all the wire to the frame.

You can, however, see the top triangle sticking out over the door frame.

Something I did not take pictures of, but I think is very important was we took steps to strengthen the door.

In my opinion, there is no sense in making a hardened building with a weak door. A door is only as strong as its frame. If the only thing holding my frame in the cement dome was a couple inches of pipe hanger strap, then a few blows with a sledge will take it out.

Once the door frame was mounted in the 2x6 frame, we drilled several 3/8 holes through the outer and inner frame. Next we threaded long (over a foot long) carriage bolts and bolted the two frames together using a large washer and a locking nut. We then threaded on other nuts and sandwiched in more large washers on the bolts to give purchase to the cement. We also invested a lot of rebar tie wire to connect the long bolts to the fencing and poultry netting. Our hope is that the cement will bond to the bolts as it does with rebar so that the door is integrated with the cement dome.

7

ADDING FERROCEMENT

I shot a video of this to explain the process:

- https://youtu.be/i-ujBh-s-Vg

This was the hardest part of the entire project so far. This was my first attempt at working with cement (other than using a couple bags of ready mix to set fence poles). To make matters worse, We were being filmed by a crew from Doomsday Preppers so we were on an extreme time limit (basically we had one day to do all the cement work), I only had one helper (Thanks Dad), and my mixer kept breaking (note to all owners of a harbor freight mixer, use locktite)...

All in all, I am pleased with the outcome, and learned a lot about what to do, what not to do, and how I would do it if I ever do it again....

What we did up to this point was to build out dome and frame in the door. Now we have to prepare for the cement.

Our intent is to cover the dome using a concept called ferro-cement (FC). In ferro-cement you don't have to use as much cement to cover a structure because you are using more structural wire, the ideal is chicken wire every ¼ inch or stucco mesh.

In most instances of using FC workers use a thick mix of Portland cement and sand 1/3 ratio, and work against each other to press a low slump (little water) mix against the wire.

This is very labor intensive, and since I just did not have time, I contacted Nolan Scheid from MortarSprayer.com[1]. His air powered sprayer really saved the project.

I will say, that in my ignorance I did most everything wrong at LEAST once, but his Sprayer enabled me to complete the job on time (well, that and my Dad's labor)

I don't want this article to sound like an advertisement for his sprayer, but I cannot express how vital it was to this process.

That being said, since my budget was too small to afford stucco mesh or enough chicken wire to wrap it 4 times to get the ¼ inch between wires, and I did not know about spider lath[2] at the time of my project, I was worried about the sprayed cement blowing through the wire. (I learned later that it depends a lot on your technique).

So I listened to my father and allowed my fears to modify the plan somewhat by adding some surplus billboard tarps[3] I bought online these tarps are old vinyl billboards and are extremely thick and durable. I originally got these for a pond project, but I was too lazy to hand dig it. I think I got them for under $30.

My original plan was to wrap the dome in welded wire fencing, then the tarp, then the chicken wire, but on site, we began over thinking and changed to covering the frame with the tarp, then fencing, then the 1 inch poultry netting. The thought was that this would allow the cement to get the benefit of the extra iron in the fencing. This caused problems when we started spraying (more about that later).

The way we used the fence wire was to divide the ground perimeter of

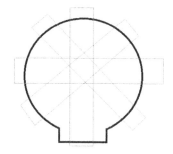

the dome (54 feet) in half and cut the welded fencing wire into 27 foot (plus a little extra) sections. We allowed the wire to roll back up into a loose roll. Next we bent one end back about 6 inches, pressed it under the base of the dome, and the used long poles to push the roll up and over the highest point of the dome.

We did this several times, each time pushing several inches of each end under the base of the dome to give us attachment points when we pour the slab.

We also pulled the fence wire as tight as we could to keep it tight against the dome frame.

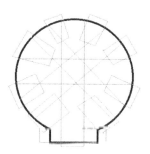

We cut left over fencing wire into 5 or 6 foot lengths and attached that wherever the long rolls did not overlap. We used rebar wire tires to tightly attach it.

We also took a section about 15 foot long and rolled it over the door frame section to make and "igloo" type door.

It was hard to keep everything tight and round, my Dad did a wonderful job of pressing down on the raised sections using a 2x2ft section of plywood and tied everything down smooth while perched on a walk-board. (I blame my dislike of heights on watching too much MacGyver in middle school)…

Next we wrapped one 55 foot length of fence wire around the base, and the forced it to fit the frame. The wire will want to stand straight up, but the dome slopes inward.

It took a lot of fighting and much wire to get the wire nice and flat.(we used a whole 1000 tie bundle of rebar wire ties on this small dome.)

You cannot tell the work put into making the dome smooth with the finished project because of the burlap roles that are supposed to "camouflage" the building, but when we do the inside, the work will show in a much smoother surface.

Next we wrapped the entire dome in Chicken wire, doubling it up so as to get as close as we could to a wire every ¼ inch.

It took us two full days to get to this part. It should not have taken this long, but we had to work with the film crew. They wanted to reshoot several key parts over and over to give the editors things to work with. (I am not complaining, just giving an overview of why a 1 day job took 2.) We did get to mix ONE load of cement that first day. I must admit, that that was the first time I had ever mixed cement, and was unfamiliar with how to use a cement mixer, the result would have been comical, if I was not worried about not getting the dome done in the time allotted. (note: I was not worried about finishing the dome, I knew that would happen. I just did not want the film crew to leave and have it edited to look like a failure).

Luckily for my stress level, the next day the film crew had to film someone else, leaving my Dad and I one whole day to work the cement.

Unfortunately we had to hash out the stress of the previous day before starting to work, and my mixer broke after just a couple of batches. (While the instructions on the Harbor freight mixer do not mention it, put Loctite and a lock washer on the driveshaft that runs the actual mixer barrel, both sides).

Being out in the COUNTRY going to the nearest hardware store took an hour and a half, during which time, my Dad hand mixed the cement to the specifications mentioned on Nolan's Mortar Sprayer website. His cement mix worked MUCH better than mine.

We were able to spray the concrete using the sprayer, and it saved our bacon, but as I mentioned earlier my change in the structure caused problems when we began to spray. What happened was that any cement that blew through the wire (I started with too the PSI set too high, and did not have the sprayer close enough to the wire). The cement then collected on the tarp causing it to bulge out away from the wire. I should have gone with the original plan of laying the tarp over the stronger welded wire fencing and just using the chicken wire for reinforcement. It would have worked better, and the conduit dome frame could have been removed later.

If found that by getting closer to the wire, more stuck to it, but since I was running out of time, and because the camera crew wanted the dome to be camouflaged to look like a boulder (Hey look, a boulder. I wonder how it got the skylights, solar panels, and big metal door...) I wrapped burlap into the chicken wire which helped catch the sprayed mortar. it also allowed me to sculpt the dome so that it had "wrinkles" and boulder like features. This did have an effect on the strength of the dome, but after the dome cures, I will tear out the tarp and spray and plaster the inside of the dome with more cement so that I get more cement into the wire. Hopefully this will make up for the strength I lost.

Luckily we were able to get everything done in time, because while I thought I would have Friday morning to do any last minute tough ups, the film crew hired a painter to paint the dome like a boulder.

He did a great job, and used all sorts of nice grey shades, so instead of a nice cement grey "boulder" we have a nice painted grey "boulder"

I don't want to sound snarky though, because I really am happy with the project, and once I get a round "tuit" and finish the dome, I think it will make a great small classroom for when my range gets built, as it is very close to where we will set up our pistol range.

Until that happens, it gives me a lockable space to keep tools and camping materials for when we spend time on the property getting it ready.

8

EXTRA ITEMS

Water Bottle Skylight

Before we added the chicken wire (which I found that professionals call poultry or avian netting), we installed the two skylights.

(The picture shows a bottle that is not full enough. In actuality the bottle works best completely full, but probably not in the winter if you have hard freezes).

The bottles don't look all that nice, and I got a lot of questioning glances from both the film crew and my Dad (he is a perfectionist when it comes to building), but when the cement dried, and we took off the plastic bags we put on it while spraying cement, they were all amazed at how well it worked.

I have a video showing the process on Youtube: https://youtu.be/M1vZSE7aPJ0

Conduit for Later Wiring

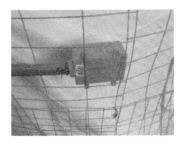

We also took the time to install plastic conduit so that we can come back later to run electricity to the building. When we made the door, we build an 'igloo' style door to create a roofline.

I plan on eventually adding a solar panel to that roofline, but My dad wants to put it on a moveable stand so it can track the sun. He is probably right, but I think my way will look cooler – In the end, we will probably make a stand.

Rain Catchment System

The last adventure in building gizmos was to create a "rain catchment system".

The Doomsday Prepper guys were the big push for this. I was not really sold on the idea, but I like to please, especially when someone else is buying the materials.

In doing my ferrocement research I found a cool website where a guy added planters[1] to his dome (this is an awesome idea and is worth a look). I figure that if my rain catchment system fails (and since it is not level it WILL fail). I will use it to plant blackberries or Muscadine grapes to cover up the dome, even though I will have to be careful about the plants creating cracks in the dome.

Having vines growing up over the dome will help camouflage it, because you can see the dome off of the Natchez Trace Parkway, a big grey "bunker" is not really that covert.

Doomsday Preppers

If you want to see the actual "dome of doom" video that Nat Geo shot of my dome build, it is on youtube:

- https://youtu.be/HF_XmwpvBxk

Additionally, I tried my first google hangout after the show aired and I talked about how the reality show process impacted my build. It is also on youtube:

- https://youtu.be/ePMicE-oVy4

If you are really into this doom of dome, I have a link to blog talk radio where I did a podcast on the process:

- https://urlzs.com/xQQyJ

9

LINKS TO CALCULATORS AND RESOURCES

Z ip Tie Domes: I think this is one of the best calculators around. Also, this Tennessee based company has patented a really ingenious system of making domes. Their PVC pipe domes are very inexpensive and are easy to build.

- https://urlzs.com/6cLEs

Desert Domes is the calculator I used when making the dome in this document. I found them first when researching domes and they have a good set of tips, especially for bamboo domes.

- https://urlzs.com/TQN6B

Domerama is another mainstay in the DIY Geodome world. I have spent a lot of time on their hub connector page in search of other ways to build domes.

- https://urlzs.com/m1FaA

Geo-Dome also has a good selection of calculators, I especially like their snow and wind load calculators.

- https://urlzs.com/hzjNR

NOTES

1. Introduction to Geodesic Domes

1. https://www.bfi.org/about-fuller/big-ideas/geodesic-domes
2. ttps://www.ziptiedomes.com/faq/What-Is-Geodesic-Dome-Frequency-Explained.htm
3. https://issuu.com/golfstromen/docs/lloyd-kahn-1971
4. https://www.lloydkahn.com/

2. Introduction to Ferrrocement

1. https://www.itacanet.org/ferrocement-water-tanks-and-their-construction/
2. http://adkison.name/ferro/ferro_cement_basics.html
3. https://theconstructor.org/concrete/ferrocement-in-construction/1156/
4. https://en.wikipedia.org/wiki/Ferrocement
5. ferrocement.com
6. http://ferrocement.com/intro-Ferro/intro.en.html
7. https://www.mortarsprayer.com/

3. Introduction to Latex Cement

1. https://www.researchgate.net/publication/295675998_Disposing_Waste_Latex_Paints_in_Cement-Based_Materials_-_Effect_on_Flow_and_Rheological_Properties
2. https://www.tngun.com/how-to-build-a-paintcrete-roof-outhouse/

4. Preparing EMT Conduit Spars

1. http://www.desertdomes.com/tips.html
2. http://www.domerama.com/fabricating/making-the-struts/geodesic-dome-struts-flattening/
3. http://www.desertdomes.com/tips.html

5. Assembling the Basic Dome

1. https://www.monolithic.org/products
2. http://www.stuartmcmillen.com/blog/chilling-domes-physics/

7. Adding Ferrocement

1. http://www.mortarsprayer.com/
2. http://www.mortarsprayer.com/spiderlath/
3. http://www.billboardtarps.com/

8. Extra Items

1. http://harmoniouspalette.com/BuildGreen.html

PLEASE REVIEW

Please visit my Amazon Author Page at:

https://amazon.com/author/davidnash

if you like my work, you can really help me by publishing a review on Amazon.

The link to review this work at Amazon is:

https://www.amazon.com/review/create-review?asin=B07W8QD45H

BONUS: EXCERPT FROM 21 DAYS TO BASIC PREPAREDNESS

There are quite a few schools of thought when it comes to personal disaster preparedness. The largest seems to be concerned with "Stuff". I call this the government model. In this model, practitioners buy gear to solve problems. They seem to feel that money equals solutions.

While you do need to have some level of resources, I feel this is a mistake, because stuff can get stolen, damaged, or lost. If you rely solely on gear, then no matter how redundant you think you are, you still have a single point of failure.

I believe in a balanced approach. In this document, I will illustrate basic concepts for disaster preparedness as well as give you some solid tips and steps to help you begin to prepare.

There is very little in the way of gear acquisition written in the following pages. You will need to acquire some measure of food, water, and equipment if you are to become more disaster resilient, however, there are multitudes of resources on and off line to help you do just that.

What is this book is designed to do is to guide you through the first steps of personal preparedness, i.e., "getting your mind right". I find that without a solid set of guideposts, it is easy to fall down the rabbit hole and concentrate only on buying stuff, or gaining training. Both of which are necessary, but neither will allow you the flexibility to adapt, improvise, or overcome.

Venn diagram of the relationship between skills, stuff, and training

I want you to be balanced, to have the right mix of things *and* skills with a strong mindset to be able to thrive in any situation.

I do not have all the answers, but I have spent decade's figuring out the best solutions for my family. Everything I wrote here are things I have done, and it has worked well for me. Take it as a guide and a starting point, question everything, and find your own solutions.

I have taken the liberty of writing this as if we were sitting in your living room talking; it is informal because preparedness does not have to be stressful.

Please do not mistake my familiar terms for ignorance of the subject. I have a degree in Emergency Management, hold certification as Emergency Management Professional, and have over a decade in planning and teaching Emergency Management in state service as well as a lifetime of doing this with my family.

If you like this Introduction to 21 Days to Basic Preparedness, you can find it on Amazon.

ALSO BY DAVID NASH

Fiction

The Deserter: Legion Chronicles Book 1

The Revolution: Legion Chronicles Book 2

The Return: Legion Chronicles Book 3

The Warrior: Legion Chronicles Book 4

Homestead Basics

The Basics of Raising Backyard Chickens

The Basics of Raising Backyard Rabbits

The Basics of Beginning Beekeeping

The Basics of Making Homemade Cheese

The Basics of Making Homemade Wine and Vinegar

The Basics of Making Homemade Cleaning Supplies

The Basics of Baking

The Basics of Food Preservation

The Basics of Food Storage

The Basics of Cooking Meat

The Basics of Make Ahead Mixes

The Basics of Beginning Leatherwork

Non Fiction

21 Days to Basic Preparedness

52 Prepper Projects

52 Prepper Projects for Parents and Kids

52 Unique Techniques for Stocking Food for Preppers

Basic Survival: A Beginner's Guide

Building a Get Home Bag

Handguns for Self Defense

How I Built a Ferrocement "Boulder Bunker"

New Instructor Survival Guide

The Prepper's Guide to Foraging

The Prepper's Guide to Foraging: Revised 2nd Edition

The Ultimate Guide to Pepper Spray

Understanding the Use of Handguns for Self Defense

Note and Record Books

Correction Officer's Notebook

Get Healthy Notebook

Rabbitry Records

Collections and Box Sets

Preparedness Collection

Legion Chronicles Trilogy

Translations

La Guía Definitiva Para El Spray De Pimienta

Multimedia

Alternative Energy

Firearm Manuals

Military Manuals 2 Disk Set

ABOUT THE AUTHOR

 David Nash is a former Marine with over a decade of experience in Emergency Management and another ten years in Corrections. He currently works in training as an instructor at a correction academy teaching new officers how to handle angry felons.

Add in a couple of semesters working in a liquor store during college and he has seen it all. In fact, David had the third highest prepper score on the NatGeo show Doomsday Preppers as well as worked more than 20 Presidentially declared disasters.

He has authored several books on preparedness, as well as worked on several disaster response plans as a state planner.

He is a father and a husband. He enjoys time with his young son William Tell and his school teacher wife Genny. When not working, writing, creating content for YouTube, playing on his self-reliance blog, or smoking award-winning BBQ he is asleep.

amazon.com/author/davidnash

facebook.com/booksbynash

youtube.com//tngun

goodreads.com/david_allen_nash

twitter.com/dnash1974

instagram.com/shepherdschool

pinterest.com/tngun

Made in the USA
Monee, IL
27 January 2024